Last supper of the senses

ALSO BY DEAN KOSTOS

POETRY

The Sentence That Ends with a Comma (1999)
Celestial Rust, a chapbook (1994)

COEDITOR

Mama's Boy (2000)

Last
Supper
of the Senses

Dean Kostos

SPUYTEN DUYVIL
New York City

ACKNOWLEDGMENTS

Thanks to the editors of the following magazines
in which some of the poems in this book first appeared:

Anthropophagy: "A Day in Guëll Park" & "Prometheus"
Art and Understanding: "Hiding in Intervals"
Big City Lit: "The Heart of the Dauphin"
Blood & Tears: Poems for Matthew Shepard (anthology): "In His Name"
(The original title has been changed.)
Bloom: "Magus"
The Charioteer: "Panayía" and "Immanent Leopard"
Chelsea: "Corot's Red Fleck" & "Gate of Ivory, Gate of Horn"
Mondo Greco: "The Blue Pause"
The Morpo Review:
"Hand" & "Spoken Under Hypnosis:
An Earlier Life in Burma as a Woman Named Mi Aye"
Rattapallax: "Golden Mouth"
Sensations Magazine: "Hera Rises from Her Jacuzzi," "Impostors of Light," & "11"
"Gate of Ivory, Gate of Horn" was a semifinalist in the
Lyric Recovery Competition at Carnegie Hall.

With great pleasure I express my gratitude to Molly Peacock, Jaime Manrique, Alfred Corn, Susan
Wheeler, Richard Howard, Constantine Contogenis, Christina Davis, Gretchen Primack, Walter
Holland, Malcolm Farley, Karen Neuberg, Penelope Karageorge, Sharon Olinka, and Darielle
Rayner for their invaluable feedback. And special thanks to Tod Thilleman.

I would also like to thank the trustees at Yaddo, where many of these poems were written.

§

"For Sight inherits beauty, Hearing sounds,
The Nostril sweet perfumes,
All tastes have hidden rooms
Within the Tongue; and Feeling Feeling wounds
With pleasure and delight: but I
Forgot the rest, and was all sight, or eye."

—Thomas Traherne

For my mother
Sofia

Part I

Part II

Part I

Taste

Taste

"All tastes have hidden rooms
Within the Tongue."
—Thomas Traherne

It's Sunday or is it sundae? I'm always hungry
    for sweets, especially chocolate—
        roan foal leaping into my mouth.

Today I ask the colt
    for a ride to the creamy language
        of yesterday and find

myself saddled to his back, past the steppes
    of Central Asia, arriving in Russia—
        time zone: tomorrow.

As the colt caracoles
    then slows, I'm aware of taste
        draining from my palate.

I bend down, look for it in the tongues
    of my shoes, not roan
        or roam but cordovan—no matter,

any brown reminds me of chocolate
    and the tingling loss
        on my wandering tongue.

The road curves and tapers. Will it lead
    where gustation has flown? A pigeon
        the color of Chekhov's hair

lands on a branch to sip dew.
    "Have you seen my sense of taste?"
        I ask. "Have you plucked

its ribbon for your nest?"
    The bird *whiffle-whiffle*s
        into a cherry orchard.

Maybe my sense is there. Clusters,
      voluptuous and crimson. Where else
            would taste vacation?

I stomp through the field
      of stumps—each one
            like Philomela's tongue—

then *whiffle-whiffle* again. Which tree?
      Which cluster? I listen to the *langue*
            of my going, the voice of not knowing

my path and arrive at a Fabergé tree: pressing
      on its trunk, I'm ushered
            through a trapdoor.

No one's inside.
      Padding into room after upholstered
            room, I hear *whiffle-whiffle*

in my head until arriving at a chamber
      with a mahogany throne. No, not wood—
            chocolate. I plunge into its cushion

and from its armrest, break
      off the carving of a pigeon
            that soars into my mouth—

Mmm . . .

Magus

I

All things in miniature to love:
a cupboard's shelves arrayed with Delft,
a green felt settee on feral
feet, the effigies of us:

homunculi who lived in dwarf
décor—rubber skin,
mouths tasting air,
scalps with holes awled in rows

as though for planting, tendrils
sprouting. I combed, curled, sprayed,
shook a doll back and forth
to relish the hiss of curls—lashed

lids blinking, the doll thinking:
What are you doing to me?
I'm a friend of your family,
I thought back.

II

"I'm a friend of your family," a thin
woman announced, meeting me after school.
With bisque skin and eyebrows
penciled into commas, she spoke

little as she drove to her clapboard house
and smuggled me up musty stairs
to an attic realm of dolls—hundreds
fanned out on shelves:

startled, drowsy, dazed in cambric
and onion-colored lace. I fell
asleep beneath their blinking eyes
as beneath a stipple of stars.

Voices tumbled toward me,
umbels of ash dissolving
at the touch of boy flesh, "Wake up,
it's time to go back to your mother."

III

Back home. All things in miniature to love
for the grown things they might become. Father
to adult puppets, and also their child, I
grew them as they grew

into me. Together in our cinder-block
cellar—flanked by angels, clowns, kings—
I sewed and glued costumes,
crowns, wings; scored and daubed

holiday tableaux for my family.
As my hands filled torsos
with vertical life, fire-
red curtains parted into hair;

my head rose like a harvest moon.
Spiraling from vinyl grooves, actors'
voices conjured seasons.
Inside those words both said and sung

—as my hands waltzed inside shadowy
puppet-sleeves—I heard, "Magic
boy, you can grow yourself up,
the night sky blooming cups of flame."

Dreaming a Last Supper

"And the sauce of the 'Last Supper' tasted of tears."
—Mina Loy

Ranks of flambeaux light the chapel of Magi Kings.
A maître d' in a priest's vestment sings,
"I'll escort you to your table." A succession of wing-

shaped screens snaps open and shut
as we pass tables draped with shrouds (shade of soot),
reserved with name cards. Without

walking far, I arrive at my chair, thank the acolyte,
and ease into my seat. The cursive graphite
on my card spells: *Nirvana.* Buddhist or Eremite?

Presto! A waiter bends in half: onto the tablecloth
he places a plate gilt with a growth
of flames coiling tail-to-mouth.

As suspense ignites, music
surges from the organ: an oneiric
requiem, cracking air with static

veins of lightning. A char scent rises from the nave.
Three waiters appear, each one balancing an empty tray
on which sits the Zen koan: pith of man or void flambé?

7 × 7th Avenue

Late-day sun is eating the Empire
State Building. As I walk from work,
I watch the glare tear off
a bite. Twilight dissolves.
A lit spirit-structure
returns, looms over the city.
Will love recast itself

into the edifice of Yes?
No, the tug of wanting-
not-wanting rearranges
"you" versus "I" in sarcophagi—
ancestors of *sarcasm*,
for insults chew
the muscled *sarx* of heart.

Home.
Snippets of things you said cling
like cat fur to sweaty skin.
My mind is a black cat leaping
across fire-escapes.
I escape into want:
a phone rings, heat

coiling through cords:
a voice purrs, "Pretend
I'm a panther's tongue."
Receivers inhale night,
exhale dawn.
(Us. Us. Susurrus.)
Day filters ore through Levolors.

Wanted-but-did-not-get
clogs the way I hear words—
anyone's: a ragged man
at the laundromat, a leafy woman
at the grocer's. My animus
billows—a resinous bubble.
Pop...

Hardening into armor, it chokes my pores
like gold body-
paint on a Vegas showgirl
who forgot to leave a patch
of naked skin for breath.
A million stomata mouth:
I thought that worship could be love.

I thought that war ship could be love.
Heading home tonight, I stop
before the grocer's bins:
a phalanx of past lovers' faces fits
round the peppers, onions, artichokes,
the plums, bananas, blood oranges...
Reach down and bite—

Sight

Sight

In an old deli—walls covered in crazed tile—I watched
    Keystone Cop movies; suddenly the actors peeled
        themselves from the screen,

reeled down my necktie, patterned
    with film frames. The black-
        white images knocked over boxes

of cakes, plates of salami;
    scampered away to look
        for meaning, believing friction

against the iris should result in *Ah-ha*
    in the heat coils of brain.
        But because I enjoyed looking

for the pleasure of seeing, sight
    considered itself wasted on me
        and secreted farther away while I

leaned over a white tablecloth,
    slurping borscht. Little did I know
        this dissolution was flooding away all

color; all images left my eyes. As I could
    no longer read, rushing October
        winds thrummed my portals

as if I were a flute.
    Become flute music—
        wind's metaphor—

I drifted over frontiers, landed
    in Bruges, velvety name like *bruise*.
        Passersby came to inspect me

as I stood near an abandoned chocolate
     factory, smelling of ghosts
          called Fumes. Then I heard

a fountain's giggling and women
     discussed unpinning coiffures
          so the tendrils could root

in groundwater where my sight
     had swum and sunk. The women
          saw in me a fellow mourner

and asked, "Why are you so sad?"
     "I'm falling into the pits
          of my pupils, where blackness

gets blacker."
     "Don't worry, we're weeping
          to rinse your eyes," they said,

telling how my necktie
     had lost its pattern, how colors
          marbleized the fountain's water.

They stirred their thirty fingers
     through currents as they sang.
          Pictures appeared:

oil paintings, photographs,
     Keystone Cop movies. With a flush
          of beet my eyes bled

their darkness away. I saw
     the three women coil
          wet hair back onto their heads;

I saw the crinkle of their green gowns
     as the sky
          thrilled aquarelle.

The Blue Pause

We studied the old farmhouse as if reading it—
our easels triangulated into dirt, the scorch
of cadmium yellow and alizarin
crimson scrawling through the leaves.

> "Notice the negative space, the pauses
> between thing and thing," is how I recall
> my art teacher's instruction. That day
> that pause was blue
> scumbled with creamy ochre—
> the sun an implication in sky, October
> tumbling behind us.

I began to see colors inside non-
color—the vermilion undersong
of weathered gray siding, the slant
of veridian in the eaves.
And, like a child taught to read
a new language, I learned the slurred
syntax between word and
word, between speaker and listener—
my brush a glistening tongue.

Utrillo

would have felt at home on this autumn street:
     the stuccoed walls lead
to a twisting Tudor mews: a child plays,
     her wheel reflecting
four o'clock sun. As I round the corner,
     trees explode into
an impasto of dense flames: quince yellow
     turns to bittersweet,
turns to titian, turns to cardinal. And I—
     also painted—smear
streaks of myself on this textured canvas
     I may never leave.

Drawn by Erasure

Based on van Gogh's drawing *Sorrow*, the model
for which was the pregnant prostitute, Christine.
The two lived together but never married.

When his paint-stained hands enveloped
and made her vellum   she left years
of night where each kiss was withdrawal

Vincent wants to father me, knowing
I'll soon be a mother. How can I be a good one—
the real father's face a shadow in a tavern?
"*Salope . . . Putain . . .*" names flung

by church folk. But now this pious Dutchman
sees me as volumes and tapering shades.
With a beard as orange as his paintings, he asks to draw
me nude. I bring my knees

to breasts and rest upon the lawn, lit
apple green. Arlesian sun casts my outline
as his hand sketches. He calls the drawing
Sorrow as if that were my new name.

Lines led toward the vanishing point
desire described as a smudge
on porous paper

What I find terrifying—yes, terrifying—
is how he sobs into his camphor-
soaked pillow. Said the sanitarium doctor
prescribed it. How he howls

like a feral dog caught in a trap. How it makes
me want to rescue him—haunted
man who climbed outside his ache
to save me.

> *Between Fail and Always*
> *they waited in narrative's smear   days*
> *erasing*

A Day in Guëll Park

a park designed by Antonio Gaudí, Barcelona

A dragon's bronze snout points
        me to a grooved plateau—
    Antonio, I'm inside your brain:
  with each footfall
  your thoughts warp
around me. I see what you saw from your cranium:

an onion dome unfists a cross
        across which your name is spelled out
          in soldered rods
              frail as roach legs.

Step by moist step: hibiscus and geranium,
  tamarind and tangerine, cherimoya and lime,
olive, monkeypod,
    candle-berry, jacaranda.

Roots bolster caves.
      Majolica-encrusted columns
          buttress a balcony of palms.

Mosaics glint a splintered sun.
How your hands healed
fragments into helixes, stars.

How an artichoke dome unpeels
   itself, reveals a galaxy
      of cobalt tesserae.

The dragon inhales the enormity, a water
  goatee dripping from his chin, his paws
draping over a basin.

Counting warts on his back, I wonder: is he your *daimon*?
Will he lead me where he led
    you—through tourmaline corridors
        of art?

       As if to answer, wind gusts a geranium
          scent, a mustache-gate
             screeches open, ushers
             me through halls to terraces
                where flame-shaped cacti point
                    down to poplar rows.
          I follow the alley
        to a ribbed vault
      that devours other tourists and me
    the way the Great Fish gulped Jonah.

Children's shouts echo
       out to their mothers—
   hair rippling like Catalan flags.

       As I yowl a *canto jondo,*
          my echo swings back,
              returns me
          where I began: one foot
       outside your thoughts, waiting
      by a bald cypress
    for your *espíritu*—
  entrance become
    exit.

Scent

Scent

A man on TV speaks of spirals,
    insists the smoke twisting into my living
        room is a scarf. I resist

the idea, for people with faces made of static
    do too much hissing. I flick off
        his phiz and light a stick of Nag

Champa Agarbatti from Bangalore because the sun
    has dissolved into a skyscraper.
        Incense circles

my neck like a cashmere scarf.
    Was Static Man right, after all?
        As I luxuriate in plush,

the Agarbatti scent goes *poof*!
    Was simply feeling it
        furred at my neck enough?

In the moment of asking, scent vanishes
    from my nostrils. Victim
        of anosmesia, refugee from my past,

I go in search of scent:
    signs invite me
        to meditate. *"Satya, Sai Baba, Satya . . ."*

I chant in a saffron chamber, my cadence
    become an aural incense...
        olfactory bulbs unthrilled.

As I chant, words curl from my mouth, float
    into air then funnel into a French horn
        to teach me secret passageways

to resee the past and pass it:
     voices sing lullabies, Good
          Friday hymns, rondeaux, rock

'n' roll. Voices speak old conversations—
     others' and mine, but none
          tenders the remedy

for my sense of scent.
     Passing through brass corridors,
          I meet

a marigolded man, face blooming
     as I near: his features swim
          toward me in reflection,

vibrissae vibrate. He tells me
     to close my eyes to shut out sight.
          Inhale the world:

slices of orange demiluned
     on a brass plate from Bangalore
          tang the morning air.

Immanent Leopard

after a mosaic from the House of Masks,
Delos, Greece

The Immanent Leopard is a chiaroscuro machine
leaping inside our muscles and thoughts:
a pattern of patters—yet unseen—

its scent clings to brown grasses as it careens.
Tintoretto rosettes spark from its pistons, its coat
a pattern of patterns, yet unseen.

Like wheels, its haunches grind and slink between
the oiled leaves of waking, the dark mud slide of sleep. What
else is the Immanent Leopard but a chiaroscuro machine?

It's the beast Dionysus rides into our dreams—amphetamine
star-paste churning in his blood. Afire, afloat:
its pattern of patterns remains unseen.

With the new-moon talons of a wolverine,
it tears Is from Is-not.
The Immanent Leopard is a chiaroscuro machine,

growling, "By Mnemosyne I was, have been
and can always be summoned, but never caught. . . ."
A pattern of patterns—yet unseen—
The Imminent Leopard is a chiaroscuro machine.

Anima(l)

for Star (1985-2001)

She hunches by the window like a jewel
in a cracked Egyptian frieze, clouds

opaque as papyrus. Inhaling
the distance, her nose becomes burnished coral.

Now she smells of beeswax
and wood shavings,

but when she thinks
I've ignored her, she smells of metal

and wet pencils. As she drowses
on crinkly mementoes, I wonder

what she's dreaming.
I imagine she hears a lion-god roar:

*"When the red wing stops beating,
return to your Master."*

As if dreaming now, I see
her silhouette projected

onto the moon. I once read in a myth
that souls of the dead flock to its onyx porches

to peer on the living and guide
their arrival. When my anima

uncoils from gravity—look up and see
its contour curved in this hieroglyph:

C_{at.}

Impostors of Light

Imagine July air steaming at midnight. If you can't
     sleep, turn on the radio. A voice
will speak of the nimbus moon—
     light refracted through crystals of ice.
If you open your blinds, you won't see it
     so stalk Seventh Avenue where
tourists stream from a hotel's columns.
     As voices multiply, figures
disappear—shades seep into cracks like oil.
     Don't try to understand, keep going.
A precipice will snap at your feet—jaw
     of an underworld: teeth
and gears, cables & tendons.
     Watch a man with stained hands
work the greasy pistons. Smell the sulfur
     drone. From a cavalcade of trucks, white
tarp will stretch across the roadwork wound.
     Notice how lamps inside the tent
cast a silhouette: muscled worker with pick-
     ax. His arc of pierce & lurch will lure
your eye as he becomes an Indonesian shadow
     puppet, light spreading across
the tent's skin. Look away
     and keep your pace to come upon the nimbus
moon. Instead, you'll find bellied,
     black bags piled like slaughtered bodies.
Holes torn & gnawed
     by hand & snout. Even if you
can't understand, keep
     going. Scan skyscrapers, but don't allow
impostors to distract from the lunatic tug, guiding
     you all along. Is that it, bolted
to a Times Square Tower, smooth
     as garlic nailed to a post to ward off evil?
Come closer: bulbs blink
     & nimbus round a disc. No,
not moon—clock.

Hera Rises from Her Jacuzzi

after Polycletus' The Bath of Hera

Damn Zeus! He kept trying
to crush our marriage–calls from Gorgon
goddesses, telephone cords curling from scalps.
Things were different with Ixion—
my gentle lover. But when Zeus spied on us, he conjured
a cloud to look like me. Ixion embraced

it; Zeus nabbed and nailed him to a fiery wheel
—sun whorling through an eternal Las Vegas.
Remember that tinseled float Zeus paraded
from his black Cadillac? On a gaudy throne
he propped his newest affair. I soared
to the platform, slashed that harlot's veils

with my saber, only to find her flesh
fiberglass. Imagine—humiliated by a mannequin.
Now I've come back to Argos, back to its rivers
green with snakes; my oils perfume leaves and sky.
Nereids plunge into my despair; from its depth,
they heal me. Woven-water, their veils purl.

This is not a spa with soaps, salts, loofahs—I am
learning transparency. As the Nereids massage
a gown of absence onto me, I enter
everything like breath. Revenge trembling with mist,
I rise from foam the way Aphrodite bloomed
from the Aegean's bloody froth, red

with the severed genitals of her father.

Hearing

Hearing

The doctor said my red sweater was to blame,
    its coloratura so loud it drilled
        holes in my hearing.

"You've collected the colors pilfered
    from the gods of Water-Gurgling-in-Creeks
        where for millennia they've bent

down, sorting stones that told
    them what mortals owed," the doctor added.
        Peeling my red sweater off, inside

out, to the color of Portuguese lamentations,
    I flew east upon its music
        all the way to Bali. Shadow

puppets zigzagged against the membrane
    of a blood-orange moon.
        Because the bony shades were mute,

I heard them insist, "C'mon, scoot
    over these corrugated tin roofs.
        It's the fastest way from From to To."

My feet roved until the Temple rose
    up before me—its finial corona,
        its Chrysler Building hat,

not aluminum, but gold and listening.
    I beseeched the gods of Lost-Voices,
        of Lost-Songs, even the gods of the Inability-

to-Hear-Shoes-Crunching-Pebbles.
    Then from the Temple's funnel,
        a teal peacock-spray spewed a perfect V:

this lack of an answer was the answer
    I had prayed for: suddenly, I could hear
        crickets in a distant cage.

Miss Chang

Did she know we were watching
her hands take flight over keys?
The tapered wings soared after each other—
a blur—the seeing of sound.

As her hands took flight over piano keys,
the chords scattered black feathers—
a blur, the freeing of music.
My friend and I slipped behind the doorframe.

The chords scattered black feathers,
sleek as Miss Chang's hair—eyeliner painted into plumes.
My friend and I sipped breath behind the doorframe,
unable to move, concerti traveling through our bodies.

Sleek as Miss Chang's hair—eyeliner pointed into plumes—
her notes pocked the air with ideograms.
Stilled, we felt flourishes scrawl through our bodies,
and wondered who our music teacher was,

her notes flocking in air. *We're ideograms,*
I thought, *spelled by the practice of hands.*
Wondering who our music teacher was,
I later learned she won a competition,

and thought: *shaped by this practice of hands,*
her tapered wings chased each other
in a race with herself, and she won the competition.
Did she know I was watching?

Follicles

for Walter Holland

Snip, snip...
In mirror's stringent glare, I point
orange Fiskars close and clip
the wing-shaped curves that swoop
below my lower lip and peak into a W.

I trim the loop from jaw to maw,
from chin to cheek, but never
get the outer edge—border
between skin and whiskers—
right.

Pluck, pluck...
Tweezers uproot violators
of precision. Follicles fall
on white porcelain, coterie
of commas. Dark sperm cells.
Pith of Father.

I grimace and twist my cheek
to glimpse and uproot pale
fibrils. The goatee's
never neat enough.

Never neat enough:
trimming countless blades along the curb
before our house.

Summer. My brother and I
had different chores: the lawn
was his province,
mowed from a throne;
I edged the cross-section
of grass and sod and walked.

Snip, snip...
The oiled shears
jawed open and shut—
beak of a mechanical bird.

Twilight. My brother
had gone indoors, sat
with my parents and watched
TV, figures of blurred light
flailing against ochre walls.

But as the moist dark of Cinnaminson
descended on my task, I had
to get the edging right,
had to get Dad to beam,
"Great job, Dean."

Instead, my brother slanted his head
from the front door, "Hey, c'mon in; it's night-
time. What're you waiting for?"
But I was never done, could always find
one more blade along the concrete lip.

Clip, clip...
I stand before the mirror:
Why not shave it off?
With no façade of topiary
I'd see my father's face.

It's Nice to See You

It (lacks the wooden thud
of "d," can't sound like *id,*
the "t" more formal: a pair
of patent-leather shoes traipses glar-
ing linguistic halls, finite word.
Within those walls—not sad, not elated—
an inscrutable third
keeps pattering toward some unstated
destination, an impersonal voice
never heard, only the plosive noise
of tongue-tip to teeth, naming the pro-
noun arriving in the antechamber of no
antecedent where it)
isn't.

Two Columns of Wallace and Emily

Let be be finale of seem—
sky the color of mimeograph paper:
flat repetitions collaged storms back—
until they gusted open ragged

seams, loosened showers of *ifs* while
bleeding into policies, blearing lines—
From the paper sepulcher of the OED,
I disinterred these Janus words:

cleave, bolt, still, fast—
floated in formaldehyde; deranged
them on the page: a white shroud—
My text is textile, weaving

Was to Am, Am to Will Be—
a seam to seal that That
entering brainwork continuously
in stabs: stitch, unstitch—

the saying always unsaid—
I drafted paper caskets, cast
Down-river where horizons
devoured. I saw them no more—

Thunderclap resounded
the clapping of hands summoned
sky's curtain to fall, dark folds
widening into a shiver of ink—

My lines crosshatched
into a scaffold of nets,
indemnity against the Fall:
this barrier against being our finale.

I could not see to see
beyond the Glass to Pine Needles;
they clattered, clawed, freeing
Mourn from Morning. There—

I witnessed Shades
iridescent as Pigeon's Neck, Fly's Face.
Scribbled by Feather, bristled Leg—
writing appeared on Misted Glass:

redemption's cuneiform
I could not understand—
scrawling through the Floorboards—
smoke from Father's hand—

how Safe to be within Walls of Stone—
to be Grackles flying through Pane
from Precinct of Snare. I returned—
a Snake's Skin, a Panicle of Ferns

wriggled within my Talons—
Talents of Domesticity and Shackles
of Smoke, Stitches and Clocks clicking
away Moons, amid conversations

with Father, chimed with the antique
Owl's *Who's Who*—
I stroked Mind's mottled Feathers—
its Patterns staining my Palms.

I blued them upon my Papers—
from Birds that Eyes have been to
wings that Hands have become—
craft a Seeing, a speaking of Be.

Touch

Touch

In rows on shelves, stacks of corduroy
      pants invite my touch—
            with/against the lines, to read them

like Braille. The nap silvers into colors:
      pewter, chain mail, sap green, phthalo blue.
          Ph . . . th . . .

Considering the diphthongs,
      I muse on their stems.
            "Φ, θ," I murmur, not thinking

of pants but of texture. How to speak it?
      A salesman asks, "*Est-*
          ce que je peux vous aider?"

"*Oh non, monsieur, je regarde seulement.*
      Mais, pourquoi est-ce que vous êtes
          speaking French?" I ask.

"We're in *Montréal*," he answered.
      "Oh, I must have fallen asleep on the train
          for Saratoga. These pants

are attractive," I add, watching the weave go dull
      then lustrous, self-restorative as water.
          As I brush *Phi, Theta,*

sensation seeps away. "*Phi, Theta*!" I insist,
      the way Sorcerer's Apprentice Mickey
          commanded mops. But Touch will

not respond; the language I'm using is not
      its own. "*Monsieur, vous ne voulez pas*
          acheter quelque chose?" the salesman asks.

"*Non, j'ai* lost a sense, and have to find it
        before it's too late," I answer,
                then clatter down cobblestones,

bend to feel them, hoping Touch will leap up
        from the gaps. I finger cut crystal, men's
                five o'clock shadows,

the ridged legs of geese. Nothing.
        Into a miraculous cathedral:
                a stained-glass Holy Ghost

splays wings like my hands the moment Touch
        flew away. Before colonies of candles,
                women sob, children huddle

at their skirts and crutches pile up like matchsticks
        in the sanctuary of the Blessed Virgin.
                I scrape my palm over splinters

to resurrect Feeling: chafe, no sensation.
        I weave through colored rays, see twisted legs,
                bulbous sores and turn away,

embarrassed by the banality of my loss.
        A shadow flickering down stairs to an alley,
                I reach a château, its door ajar.

Has Touch hidden in a gauntlet? Creak upstairs,
        see a stained-glass panel: Goddess of Arms.
                Sunray fingers lure me down the hall

to a collection of mirrored armor
        —word so like *amour*—emotion awakened
                by Touch. Didn't Jeanne D'Arc wear

45

armor as she charged into battle, the skies aflame
      with angels? As sun squeezes through a bevel,
          it flickers onto fish-scales

of chain mail. I stroke the riveted
      rings, coax a bud of blood:
          warmth blooms into my hands.

Hand

In the midst of glass
he can't quadrate
a mannequin's hand
into its polystyrene
wrist. He can't adjust
its gesture.
The square flange
lodges in the wrist's square
hole the wrong
way, so the hand
won't rest at hips
(poised as if the mannequin
stalked breezes,
long hair scrawling
toward a future),
instead twists
forward, agitated
as if it could rip
a hunk of flesh,
as if it could
strangle him.

The Heart of the Dauphin

"This is the end of 200 years of uncertainty.
Until now, his death was stolen," Philippe Delorme.
— *The New York Times*, April 20, 2000

July 13, 1789
No, not a flower, three spurts of flame—
That's how I see the fleur-de-lis. Look:
Maman wears a diamond one
      that swims with candle stars.

Now she's playing the virginal;
can you hear? I float down a river
inside its painted lid. Her fugues
      carry me like currents. With boats

in blue coiffures, a duchess, a countess,
an empress sail by. A cage with a squawking
cockatoo roosts in a czarina's wig.
      Hems whisper names into sand

as a lady glides past the fountain—swoosh!
Dressed up as a yew, a duke holds her hand.
Maman plays a goodnight rondeau as guests
      in pointy shoes disappear

like ghosts between queues of statues:
gods with moldy faces and blank
eyes. *Maman* calls me to her, "Swim
      off to bed, my little dolphin."

While I watch from my bedroom window,
Nounou knocks at my door: "Charles Louis . . ."
She tilts a plate of petits fours, each masked
      with the face of an animal.

I sink into my canopy bed—its lilac-scented
sheets printed with crowns—and chew

an apricot lion, a ginger giraffe,
        a crème de menthe dolphin.

July 14, 1789

Pamphlets flurry streets:
What is The Third Estate? Everything.
What has it been till now? Nothing.
        What does it seek to be? Something.

"We pay the poll-tax, the salt-tax, the tithe;
we swell the wealth of the Crown; we
eat scraps too small for cockroaches,"
        the Jacobins shout.

Wearing a cockade of horse chestnut leaves,
a man climbs atop a barrel and calls, "To arms!"
The mob hells, strips gunsmiths and Les Invalides
        of muskets and cannons. The herd

clamors toward La Bastille: its crenelated
towers point long shadows to imprisonment
and executions without cause,
        to *lettres de cachet.*

October 5, 1789

Thousands of women clang sabers and pikes,
and march to throw *Maman* from her throne.
The racket grows and even though I cover my ears,
        it hammers into my head.

January 21, 1793

L'Hôtel de Ville: prelates and nobles stand around Father
in bright robes; the Third Estate wears black. Marat
and his men drag Papa off to the prison of *Le Temple.*
        Please, please don't hurt him—

July 2, 1793
Explosions of glass—I bolt up in bed. "Why,
Maman?" Men with square hands burst
into Le Trianon, smash open the gilt
          doors. The men stink

so much I can't breathe. Oily grime on necks
and clothes. A man shouts, "We are
The Committee of Public Safety." They tear
          Maman from me and tease,

"Dauphine, Dauphinette—Go ahead, tell us you hate
that perfumed bitch, Madame Déficit!
Her porcelain maw, a sow's vulva. Say it
          to save yourself." No. . . .

A man strokes our brocades, gazes into mirrored
galleries, ogles his reflections. Turning,
he turns into a gargoyle—talons hook me
          like a suckling pig:

"Your mommy's powdered neck, her horse-
hair, whore-hair curls. Her head will dance
through streets of Paris on a spike—
          Come watch, my little dolphin boy!"

Another man hacks off the coat-of-arms
with three interlocking dolphins, lugs it away.
Blindfolded, in back of their curtained carriage,
          I hear the men sing:

          Veux-tu connaître
          Un cocu, un bâtard, une catin?
          Voyez le Roi, la Reine,
          Et Monsieur le Dauphin . . .

The eyeless ride brings me to *Le Temple*. No
temple, no place for gods or humans. Where is
Maman? Who'll take care of me now?
          No, no, no throbs from the ache

where the men smashed out my teeth. Panic
swells and sticks to my skull. I fall and
fall into a hole of sleep. One, two, three days pass.
        Red rat eyes puncture the dark,

then dart as keys jangle. Men guffaw, their voices
reek of wine and sulfur. One man bites breath
from my mouth. Others rip the ragged clothes
        from me: I am Versailles.

Clutching candles, they eye the conquest: a man shoves
my face to the floor, hurts my bottom with jabs.
In their laughter, I black out. Shadows the shape
        of hands swarm over me.

October 21, 1793
Guards brag that a pack stacked a pyramid
of 2,800 heads, that a ghoul balanced *Maman's*
head on top, crimson crusting her cheeks.
        Listening, I weep blood—

1794
Archives insist I live at *Le Temple*
two years. Don't believe those brittle books.
I tell you it's longer, tell you those men
        (except one, who grows

to love me) return less often, afraid
of tumors gnarling my legs, of scabies,
of vermin. I rasp my skin open
        to soothe the sores.

If only *Maman* would return to me. . . .
I lie on this mattress of gnawed
straw, hating my stench on the blanket.
        She appears:

In the dark, her eyes are eyes of rats.
I raise a torch and see her water-colored
iris, her coral mouth, her meringue hair
        writing into white

snakes that twist from her scalp. *Maman,*
your pupils become embers as you
chant this rondeau: "One heart
      we had betwixt us twain;

Which being dead, I too must *dree.*
Death, or like carven saints we see.
In choir, sans life to live be fain,
      Death!"

But she's only a head lanced on a spike. Rank
after rank of stakes with her head
file by—a choir of faces on fire—
      my cell grown vast

as the Grand Ballroom. When I wake, her face
liquefies. Morning trickles into my cell
through a crack where Marat's men
      sealed my window. Sucking

out my breath, this room is a rancid mouth
I rot inside. Try, try, try to chip
the mortar without the guard hearing—
      My fingers bleed.

Each night the pageantry comes back:
the eyes white-hot, a black sap drips
from lips. One night—I'm not sure how—
      it rains inside my cell:

Fat drops of molten bronze! Hundreds
slant down in phalanxes, become scorpions
digging into my scabs, my tumors.
      Stingers pierce me.

I see their bruised and powdered faces:
tout chacun c'est le visage de Maman . . .
Embedded, the scorpions nest inside my skin.
      I talk and laugh and sing to them.

1795

Books swear I die soon after. None
agrees on the cause. Each one says I'm
only ten. And that part's true. But I'm no
      longer sure what death

spells. After all, here I am—a blur
of ether—scrawling above these words
as I once hovered above my corpse.
      Again I view

the autopsy scalpel halve my torso: ribs
splay like a bear trap. Small for my age,
shrunken by hunger, my heart
      is a prize in the eyes

of another doctor, Philippe-Jean Pelletan.
While the autopsy team dilates on opinions,
rinsing instruments, he carves it out. Wrapping
      it in a handkerchief,

he secretes the organ into a satchel, floats it
in alcohol, but doesn't press the stopper
tight. As details of my death fade,
      the alcohol spirits

itself away. My heart dries hard as *Maman's*
diamonds. For years, it peers from a fluted
jar as I now peer through ether.
      Finding a rusted key,

Pelletan's mustachioed aide-de-camp
unlocks the chained room: drowned
in shadow, a pell-mell of papers, books
      and figurines from travel

—baboon's skull, Javanese Buddha—
under a fur of dust. Coughing back
gray air, the man steals my mushroom-
      colored heart. Amulet . . .

One night, while he drowses over Voltaire,
I plunge my fist between his ribs, unstring
his heart like a harp. Arm throbbing, he grabs
      his chest, gasps and dies.

His widow, racked with guilt, drops
the amulet into a purple pouch, hangs it
from an iron fleur-de-lis before
      the house of Pelletan.

In a return to *Dieu* and *l'Église*, he
pleads it to the Archbishop: "Anoint
this as a reliquary." In prayers they revere
      this morsel of me.

1831

Hoards impale servants, jam-pack crosiers
and crucifixes into sacks. The Holy Palace
is another Versailles! I gawk—not wanting to—
      through the membrane-

lens between our realms. Hearing the uproar,
the Archbishop's printer, a certain Monsieur
Lescroart, grabs a crystal urn,
      plants my bulb

inside and stuffs the archives that attest
its authenticity into his vest. Hunting
the scentless ghost of a child, guards
      gut the palace

with bayonets, squalling like beasts.
A sentry corners Lescroart in a stairwell,
wrestles him, snaps his neck like a lily stem.
      The urn shatters

down marble stairs, where wine-light spills
from a stained-glass window. There it is—
coronated by fragments engraved with fleurs-
      de-lis: the heart, freed

from the world I knew. Imprisoned in
Bourbon beliefs—no less than in dank cells
—we justified the grief we caused
        beyond our mirrored walls.

Here, I spirit through chambers—cells
in a crystal beehive—where I see
from other bevels of view and time
        with a swarm of eyes.

April 19, 2000
Under fluorescence, Philippe Delorme
pins and clamps my antique heart, shaves it
as a chef would a truffle. He lays
        a sliver on the slide,

peers through a microscope, spies
onto another era: compared with DNA
from decayed wisps of *Maman's* hair,
        my molecules mouth what voices

long denied, what Delorme now types
on history's screen: *Charles Louis XVII, Le Dauphin.*
Two spurts of flame   *MarieAntoinetteson*
        in cosmic static fuse

Part II

Safety

Safety

As a mirror assures me the buttons
        of my double-breasted jacket line up, I reach
                deep into pockets. Empty...

A draft whistles across the transom.
        Have robbers made off with my sense
                of safety? I bolt down five flights to chase

the scream leaping from my throat and I turn a corner:
        Buddhist chanting floats from a window.
                Will I find safety here? Zooming

up the elevator, I meet people on grass mats
        who teach me to watch my breath. They name
                each thought "thought" as each one arises,

but it all requires thinking. No matter how much I think "no,"
        I can't silence my fears. The white page the instructor
                tells me to be turns Naples yellow. A woman

from a nearby mat whispers, "Alitalia has flights every hour."
        Should I go to the country whose color is the state
                of my mind? Maybe they'll know how I can

retrieve safety. Jetting from Kennedy
        to *Città Eterna*, I take the train to *Napoli*. A skinny
                boy runs past me, yellowing in my mind.

"Please, have you seen my sense of safety? I lost it
        in New York and am hoping to find it here," I say.
                "*A l'etichetta!*" the boy insists.

Etiquette? I think. Have I been rude? "*Ma scusi, ragazzo,
        non volevo essere scortese,*" I say in textbook Italian.
                "*No, signore,*" the boy responds,

"The label, look at your label." I pry back the flap
        above my heart. The label
                I hadn't noticed reads *Never Name.* "No-

w look beneath it, inside the pocket,"
        the boy explains. A vellum card reads:
                SPEAK DANTE'S LANGUAGE OF YES.

In His Name

for Matthew Shepard

The speakers throbbed with red music.
>   *He will fill your mouth with laughter,*
>   *and your lips with shouts of joy.*

"What do you want? Where can we go?"
>   *He did not create a chaos.*

They gunned the engine, wind
whipping black as they sped,
>   *and ask for the ancient paths*
>   *where the good way lies, and walk in it . . .*

passing corn and wheat and barley fields
to a threshing floor: fists
pummeled his frame, hands hammered
a pistol butt into his skull,
jeers stabbed the air, his face
collapsing on their rage.
>   *O prosper the works of hands.*

With arms roped cruciform to a rail,
with legs spread-eagled, he torqued and fell
limp. While the pupil-dark sky loomed
in witness, the light of his body dimmed.
>   *And all of us, with unveiled eyes, seeing*
>   *the glory of the Lord,*
>   *as though reflected in a mirror,*
>   *are being transformed into the same image.*

Breath wheezed through swollen nostrils
and lips—all identity crushed
but his name.

Gate of Ivory, Gate of Horn

Homer regarded dreams as dwelling on the shores of Ocean, in the extreme west. Deceptive dreams issued from a gate of ivory, true dreams from a gate of horn.

I/ Ivory

I oil the hinge so it sings
open, polish brass finials on each post,
then leave the gate ajar to entice: see

my manic lawns, my topiaries with perfect
clairvoyees, my foxglove and bleeding
hearts, my hibiscus and anthurium.

I'm proud of my gardener who clips
crescent-moon nails into soil
and charms them into whomever

one longs for, whatever one wishes to relive.
A treed alley leads to the field
where my gardener harvests the flesh

of dreams, storing it in silos. Ranks
of flowers secrete attar: *intoxicate*.
Mirrored domes glisten: *blind*.

With rubber tubes attached to the sump,
I pump the gaseous spirits of those who
lived foolish lives at my expense

then cull them into earthenware jugs and
—*glug, glug*—
pour them down Lethe's drain.

II/ Horn

It stands before our grounds like a comb
untangling strands—overgrown grasses.
We spend so much time in books and trees, we

often forget the garden. Our communal home
hums—no gardener here. We all
do our lot: the brood and elders alter greens

by the sun, a kind of photosynthesis—lights'
delicate explosions on needle and leaf.
We chant the trunks pale blue, pale blue they be.

We chant the oxen red, red they be
and we hitch our carts to them, jam-
packed with chalices and bowls, bearded

bulbs and ribbons,
letters and lockets, manuscripts never
published, paintings never shown.

Creak, creak—
we cross a bridge of woven hair
above a river of fire.

Our fleet oxen manage
to get us to the other side.
But the road was a ring all

along: we return, the grasses higher
than before. Yet our cart is so much lighter
now—the fragments of Never evered.

11

Turn off TV voices that shrill, "The Towers . . ."
Each station replays the crashes that drill The Towers.

Unclench your gaze from the belch of papers, shoes, flesh.
Blue air cracks: a fault in oblivion distills The Towers.

Ignore pleas sieved through cell phones (*Can't get out . . .*),
silenced by gases that tendril The Towers.

Don't read last words e-mailed to loved ones.
A wind of fractured phrases fills The Towers.

Reverse the plunge of bodies: linked arms are hoops
swallowing names from sills of The Towers.

Mask mouth and nose against crematorium ash; bones swim
into air. Remains hymn through nostrils: The Towers.

Undo your fascination with the looming forest of smoke.
Its milky fumes weep on the city. Will The Towers?

Walk past Xeroxed faces that altar bus stops with downloaded
prayers, our Lady of Guadalupe and daffodils for The Towers.

Ignore a man with broken teeth who totes a white bucket
of photos rescued from the smoldering hills: The Towers.

Unmangle answers as tracery façades soar
from the talus of rubble. Untwist ideas that killed The Towers.

Forget legions in medieval helmets, who probe, hack, crane—
who write white-hot with a welder's arc, signing the nil: The Towers.

Initiate

The concrete sewage pipe jutted above the creek
                near our house. I was six
years old. No more than a yard in diameter,
                the pipe stank: sour, gaseous.
Other times it omitted no odor at all,
                drawing my brother, friends
and me in like a hungry moue. We just could not
                resist. In its dark dwelled
all mystery—labyrinthine and dangerous.
                Rats' eyes eviled the black.
We shrieked back into sun and creek, out of breath. Thrilled.

O

"The eyes must reflect what is not."
—André Breton

Even a cynic—whose reason he may boast of—knows
the Known's erasure is the cost of O's.

Though prayer may not light incense to an idol,
an unsummoned answer announces the cost of O's.

Egg-like, a secret cracks in the act of writing:
text, as nest, hatches the cost of O's.

Closed eyes contain remembrance.
Each open "I," mirrored, glimpses the cost of O's.

A lone person in an audience gasps;
drunk on shadows, insight increases the cost of O's.

Are they zeros that multiply 1 into googol?
A man subtracts what is not his: the cost of O's.

Ring by ring, he climbs toward the negative space
of *not* and *no*, of all that enlarges the cost of O's.

His name is Kostos, a coat he wears over self:
He peels it off to swim toward who he is: the cost of O's.

Worth

Worth

I wear this belt tight—notches calibrated,
    each one labeled "Control."
        And when I think of the nothing I've done

and feel like a fraud, I pull
    the belt tighter, suck it all in.
        Worthlessness, like fat around the belly,

can be disguised and constrained, subverted
    and subtracted, yet always remains.
        I winch the ox-blood belt

on a flight all the way to Mexico—
    land where slaughtered sun
        bleeds over pyramids each night.

Yanking the belt, I leave welts on my waist,
    wonder how I'll rate
        in the home of Paz and Kahlo.

As nerves and umbilicus intertwine
    above her self-portrait, Frida's infant self glides
        mid-air like a space shuttle.

The painter tells me, "This was the self
    I gave birth to, a baby cooing,
        "'*Puedo.*'"

I thank her for this insight as tarantulas
    knit her eyebrows. "Sorry for having
        another appointment; I'll call you *mañana,*"

I say. Hurtling through traffic, passing cathedrals
       and pyramids, I knock on Octavio's door. He's dead,
           but makes time for me anyway. Instead

of a red carpet, he unrolls an endless scroll
       of *blanco* paper all the way down the hill
           to usher me all the way up.

Bestiary Beyond My Door

I was the boy who invented beasts

with make-believe grammar, conjured them
to mooch where fear banished me from going,

cast spells the way a sculptor casts bronze:
"Skulk of foxes, husk of hares,
clowder of cats . . ." Luxuriant manes, fur

on bellies tufted brown and gray and matted.
Flanks hung down in folds. Teaching the creatures
to take compliments, I brushed
their coats that changed from cinnamon

in summer to flecked brunette in winter.
Peering up at me, the beasts slunk against my legs:
hoofed animals, pouched animals,
meat eaters, insect
eaters, Monotremes and Howlers,

Greater Kudu, Lesser Kudu, Turs
and Audads, Kiang and Kulan
and even an Aye-aye. All wore
some part of my face. "Your markings
help you fit in. No one will know you're not
me. Go now, bring back pieces of the world,"

I yelped. But some of my kids and whelps
scattered at the approach of humans, others
attacked. "Unkindness of Pangolins, siege
of Cacomistles," the animals invoked
as they spawned offspring, breeding
beyond my control. I no longer knew them.
Grown now, I eye from my door, pine planks

worn smooth below stocking feet from years
of sentry. When my brood mulligrubs
in dank rooms, I coax them with leashes: "Go
back outside to live for me,
cells and selves fused." And my Kinkajou,
my Woolly Coendou, my White-tailed Guereza
and my Collared Partridge skirr with grinning
faces, in search of insects, fruit and sex.

Creature of Two Worlds

The landscapers rooted iron lances
deep as teeth, then planted a sapling near that fence

upon whose enameled spear a passerby
clamped a padlock. Overhead, clouds multiplied.

Rains. Parades. Funerals. Sirens.
Rust and grime fused iron to iron

as sycamore sapling became sycamore tree,
two elements forced to agree.

It became a creature of two worlds: in one, unaware
of the fence, muscling green quadrants in air;

in the other, letting crusted spears and lock
stab its trunk in a slow-motion fuck.

Despite its growth, the tree can't bend
to thrust out the obstacle, and so pretends

to need it, burling pulpy meat
over the metal like a punched lip eating.

The desire to be freed may not relent,
yet a saw would gut the core to cut the fence.

Eating God

The seed goes down, god dies,
a rising happens,
some crust, and then occurs   an eating.
                              —John Berryman

"Take, eat; this is my body, broken
for you," a priest chants as he breaks the bread.
Trying to understand, a boy peers
into the monstrance, sees language in rite
transubstantiate itself, bleed. Logos is Word,
Logos is logic to explain "theophagy."
Logos becomes mother, father, teacher, nurse.

Seeking is suckling. When the boy grows
into man, he devours temporary gods
but still can't understand, so he gnaws
books: *Bhagavad Gita, Kabbalah, Philokalia,*
the *Gnostic Gospels'* leather scrolls
in urns, dug from sands of Nag Hammadi:
I plead with you, be not an unseasonable kindness.

The man tracks history's tattooed parchment, telling
how hunters would feed on beasts to incarnate
strength of a bear, speed of a deer. And how one
person devoured another to slip into his god's skin,
to wear a crown of blasted columns. Stalking ruins
thick with thorns, the man deciphers: "History is written
in war," Herodotus then, now on CNN.

"I plead with you, be not an unseasonable kindness,"
sighs an icon, its gold-leaf skin dissolving flake
by flake into the man. Older, enlarged by loss, he leans
toward earth's hunger, swallowing teacher and votary,
preacher and nurse, idolater and freak.
From the bowels, soil leaps back, "First
you must chew your flesh into speech. Try to make it last."

Health

Health

Although the Pharos of Alexandria has crumbled,
    I follow its phantom rays through arteries
        and alleys—past ports and minarets,

past houses with *hoshes,*
    past bazaars where crops
        of land and sea heap up. Choosing

a burgundy fruit, I amble toward the city.
    Breeeeee-oooooo . . .
        A far-off signal summons my steps on,

on. Pocks and scars along the road
    harden into bridges, leading
        to Hygeia.

Under bilious skies, I cross other bridges:
    some thatched with milk thistle,
        some stained with ancient teas.

Though the sandals chafe my feet, I can't pry
    them off or stop. Eager for a cure, my liver
        becomes a verb and speaks: *Live.*

Once you tried to extinguish yourself
    like the Pharos, but neither its fuse
        nor your own could be stubbed

out. Now its skeleton light seeps
    into you as you intuit
        health. Press your lips to my stem—

breathe phosphor into my fibers.
    Hang me like a lantern
        above your life.

Writ in Water

for Agha Shahid Ali

When Keats coaxed his mind to be a page of whiteness,
he unrolled a scroll of seeing, required for witness.

Latin *spirare* blends spirit and breath.
The word *transpire* exhales as flesh expires in witness.

Knowing his breath would spiral away, Keats
gave himself to odes and sonnets, inspired to witness.

As a brede of lesions pocked his lungs, he no longer climbed
the Spanish Steps. Bedridden, he desired witness.

Each night he leaned deeper into that urn that spoke,
to learn its wordless beauty: truth lyred in witness.

Did he pour his self into the word *martyr—witness* in Greek?
Did he write his nest of poems to be pyred in witness?

Am I, Dean, too afraid to mold the dark
that surrounds the self prior to witness?

Death's negative capability reclaims the artist,
but bequeaths the art, in ink or clay—fired in witness.

Made of Blades, Your Poems Are Urns I Was Afraid

for Sylvia Plath

to get near, so in dying October light,
I drove to Smith to be near *you*:
the columns pointing skyward
like patriarchal trees, the greenhouse
fragile as a vowel, the lake a lazy

eye. I pictured you there with your
crossed-out papers, your inamorato
thesaurus; pictured you among a clutch
of pleated young women in black
and blank, cooped by a saw-toothed border.

Children cried from another room
—another time, another you—milk
bleeding from their mouths. I pictured
you alone, correcting versos, London
mist opaquing vistas past your pane.

Your hearth became a fever—gases
swarming blue tattoos into your blood,
medulla, spine: the gases sucked
your animus from bones, rendered you
flute. Your maw, cast pewter. Now

I re-see that photograph: your silhouette
leached away—an urn-shaped stain.
Outside, a night wind roils the lake,
uncoils a breath breathed in
through vowels: I owe you

Hiding in Intervals

I fled your room each time I cried,
though of course, you couldn't hear me.
(With the door closed, I cracked inside.)

I tried to compose myself, tied
up like rubber-banded daisies—cheery.
I cheerily fled your room each time I cried.

This architecture of going to hide
in intervals provided walls of safety—feeble theory!
The hospice door closed; I crumbled outside.

Five days I sat in vigil, tugged by the tides:
need-fear, need-fear, need you near me.
As in a ritual, I solemnly rose to cry,

knowing it made no sense to—your sense had died.
As if disembodied, I watched my own motions, teary-
eyed, as I closed the door and collapsed inside.

The day of morphine, you metamorphosed beside
me into an infant. Could I have cradled you more dearly?
Quitting the room and my face that lied,
I was the door *and* the man it kept outside.

Prometheus

It began iron gray, blunt
        as pain, took the shape of two hands

he called Bird.
        Ragged as the ragged

wind that bore his black outline,
        the Eagle swooped down

at night, its talons and wings,
        its beak a steel needle

shooting between ribs, slavering
        out the biopsy delicacy—

the liver a nugget of oblivion
        examined by day in the infectious

glare—shame. But the bond
        of dark and light, of need

and take inscribed itself on the whirr,
        on petals of hepatica.

Prometheus reclined on his left side,
        the tenderness on his right

a rot of shade so deep
        eternity guttered at its edges.

The collapse into unknowing
        became the god's daydream, his nude

prognosis sprawling on oily shale
        at the brink of a world.

Blood-spattered wings
        surveyed the shores each night.

Sanity

Sanity

When Aramaic seaweed scrawls across my skin,
      shoals glister by in fluent phrases, eyes
           etching mine and mind.

How can I leave?
      But the fisherman hauls me
          up, warns I'll drown

and I live with him in the confines of boat,
      shinnying up the mast like Odysseus
          to look longingly

on the sea. Yet with each salt plash, I'm committed
      to the ship's walls, planks hammered
          higher every day. My father,

the fisherman, says, "Son, it's safe here—stern
      and bow easy to see. The planks
          can be mended with nails.

When you dream the ocean, you risk
      the unfathomable. My rope may not be long
          enough to save you." So we sail

many years and pretend to be solid, the reality
      around us liquid. We spot a lighthouse
          and moor at a quay. "It's land,

logical land, Dean, it is good—you can weigh it.
      Walk with me the length of going."
          Trudging through my melancholy

weeds, we come to a cascade. "Look,"
      I say, "this is the harmony of water
          against land in give and take

with gravity, where to lose one's mind
      is to reshape it
          in a shirr of coursing glass."

Corot's Red Fleck

A man in a red coat skims a punt
across a lake, flimsy as a mosquito. As the wake
wrinkles, his cadmium coat provokes the pewter
of landscape to green—its glaze, silvered.

≈

Hold your thumb over the man who
has somewhere to go. Gone,
the greens seem less so, without their complement:
red. Instead, they sink beneath tarnish. Now
take your thumb away: again the jot incites
the green, where trees have narrative,
and hills and runnels, theirs. The fleeting figure—
always a fleeting figure, a satchel of wind
nearby—already knows the plot.

≈

In *Nadja,* an impoverished young woman weighs
slabs of meat on waxed paper. That flesh wept
red onto Breton's page as he noveled her.
Both voyeur and adulterer, guilt
was his necktie.

Glimpsed through a traction fissure, Paris
emerges as a third character in halftone photos:
the city follows Nadja madward to asylum.

Beautiful but brutal, I thought,
then reached the final page. Like Corot's
red fleck, that ending convulsed
back through the book, silvering.

Vertigo Torque

"There is no terror in a bang,
only in the anticipation of it."
— Alfred Hitchcock

While dangers threaten to enthrall,
the space below vaults up and beckons:
resist the leap, but not the fall.

What no one told her, braced against the wall,
was how the bell tower darkened.
While dangers threatened to enthrall,

its stairs writhed up into the spiral
of Madeleine's chignon. The last steps taken:
she resisted the leap, but not the fall.

What no one told Scotty, in museum halls,
was that he'd fallen for a painting—and broken.
While dangers threatened to enthrall,

the woman's hazy past had scrawled
a portrait he would try to reckon.
He resisted the leap, but not the fall.

In theater's black ocean, all
is vortex: we fight its torque, but weaken
—while dangers threaten to enthrall—
resisting the leap, but not the fall.

Love

Golden Mouth

The name Chrysostom derives from *chrysó stoma*
—golden mouth—referring to eloquence.

Rings:
>	you and Mother orbited the altar
>		three times, the priest intoned

the liturgy of St. John Chrysostom,
>	*stéphana* wedding crowns saturned
>		your heads. A satin ribbon

bound your mother-of-pearl wreaths
>	together. Rings: the mouths you pressed
>		your mouths to—champagne

flutes to drink a life from. That depth wept
>	away in years. . . . As you stepped back
>		through the shellacked door,

home from a party, the swords
>	of your words glinted
>		midair.

Your tuxedo and Mother's ink-
>	green taffeta fell to the floor.
>		In the Eros

of anger, you fathered me,
>	wearing this ring
>		that humid August night, dark

chest hair matting your skin, your bruise-
>	colored nipples.
>		And through aching

flesh—the claret of my mother—
>	I was spoken into
>		World.

Panayía

at Evangelìstria,
the Cathedral of Virgin Mary's Dormition
(Assumption), Tinos, Greece

Like opera gloves fringed in satin
blood, a saint's severed hands float toward you.

Your corpus sails
on a freshet of veils in this icon painted

with the tip of a monk's white beard.
Arriving in boats, people proclaim your death

"Great Sleep" and breathe
your prayer beneath eucalyptus trees. Your Son

no longer needs air as he
looms atop this icon's panel: straight-backed

on a settee of flames, he is
a *Pantokràtor* like none I've seen: Christ

the Mother—death fusing
Madonna into Son, fe- and male into one.

His belly is a convex window revealing
his womb: palming from inside its pane, a child-

you mouths words I can't hear.
What are you trying to tell me? I stalk

this gallery of icons—painted
moments lined up in a sequence of freeze-frames—

stop at the instant before infant Jesus
left your womb: his hand—pink beak of fingertips—

already blesses. Not pacing
toward but from, I come upon another icon. St. John

the Baptist roosts on a cliff,
his future coursing from his neck: rinsed

by his own dying,
his head smiles like a conch. Finally I arrive

at your weeping icon:
healer of the crippled, the wheezing, the barren.

"Parthèna . . ." "Platitèra . . ."
"Panayìa . . ." The many names

summon your realm to ours.
Now a rose-scented sap streaks this glass

that guards your face
from time's discolorations. An opal blur arcs

above your shoulders:
Heaven painted with just one hair.

Spoken Under Hypnosis:
An Earlier Life in Burma
as a Woman Named Mi Aye

Imagine stepping through a gate that is exit and entrance:
pass from who you are to who you could
no longer be. What do you see?

Pretending not to notice men's glances,
    I traipse, soles tasting soil.
        Filaments I embroidered

into dragons entwine on the *longyi* skirt
    whispering across my calves.
        Lanterns yaw overhead. Pushed

by the crowd, a soldier falls into me—
    The way a blade slices an envelope,
        he opens my silence.

      What does he say?

He calls my eyelids *suede seeds*,
      my hair *black streams*. His arms gleam
        like leaves after rain.

By candle-flicker, my hair scrawls calligraphy
    onto his chest. He leaves, but always returns
        until the moon no longer bleeds persimmon.

My belly swells like a rice sack.
    While another life ripens, I grow
        thin. Can't eat. Food reeks.

I'm a door closing, a door against.
    Not wanting to shame Mother,
        I spill air from my veils and sail

into a ravine. In brief oblivion, my silks and hair
      tint a cut of sky. When spasms
           cease, she holds the baby: bald squab,

flesh flinching against death. She wraps it
      in banana leaves,
           buries it by the creek.

What do you see now?

Mother wakes me with a bowl of rice
      but it looks like maggots—
           My arms go cold, my self coils

from its core. I lift from flesh: pit from fruit. She
      spreads my cloths across her pillow, entombs
           her face in embroidered leaves. . . .

What do you see after dying?

Petals hover in hoof-smoke as a gold
      Buddha riding a gold throne
           sails men's shoulders on a palanquin.

A basket swells with saffron rice; another spills
      pomegranates and lotus pods the color
           of oxblood. Binding my days to Eternity,

an altar wears a swag of knotted ropes.
      A man tilts a mirrored disc—plate full of sky—
           a boy breathes into an oliphant,

an elder thrums a boat-shaped harp; from its strings,
      dead ancestors sing me toward them,
           our words dissolve like gauze.

Are you at peace?

I can't say; peace no longer has an opposite.

Laundry: A Meditation

I

Watch selves twist through a washing
machine's circular window:
how a T-shirt's neck yawns, how seams
of a robe narrate a nun's shoulders. Soap scent
recalls the memory of a rose-
aroma that escaped from St. Claire's pores
as she lay beneath a domed, crystal
lid, her flesh dry as cigar leaves.

After her death, Michelangelo
spent months at a time, supine
on a scaffold, daubing muscular
clouds to wrestle back heaven,
shoes rotting onto his feet.
He peeled their hide from his own
while Adam's fuse-finger ignited
Dominus across dominions of plaster.

II

Gazers aim their chins to take in
Baroque pageantry. Sunlight rinses
the frescoed hordes above, coaxing a figure
to live: Apostle Bartholomew's arm
holds the draped gown
of his flayed skin; hands and face sag,
mouth gaping:
WHO?

Was this Buonarroti's self-fresco,
like his self-sculpture in the *Unfinished
Pietà?* He becomes a marmoreal monk,
a breast-shaped hood covering his head.
Though we can't see his face, the broken
nose identifies him. He props up two mourners
who cradle the body deposed from the Cross
the way spirit mothers matter.

III
Smoothing out a dried T-shirt, I find stigmata
no bleach can efface, pull the garment
over my head, onto my chest, reveal the stain:
I am.

Love

I hate to do laundry.
    As soon as I'm finished, it needs
        doing again, especially underwear.

To stretch the cycle, I've become a collector:
    briefs, boxer-briefs, boxers—some white,
        some the gray of tarnished mirrors.

The satchel swells, the supply dwindles:
    back to the laundromat.
        Folding the underwear on a counter—

plain and sexy ones piled together—I fantasize
    someone undressing me;
        Callas sings *Non Credea Mirarti*

as our clothes fall to the ground. I find myself
    transported; with a voice
        less plangent than Maria's, I croon,

watering geraniums on a balcony in Nafplio
    —medieval town in modern Ελλαδα—
        its stone walls like wool, its terracotta

roofs a weave of russet. Maria's sleepless ghost
    bends from her window across the courtyard,
        leans into her sorrow,

learns to trill again
    from canaries, the way she did as a girl,
        fingers pressed to their throats.

A blue jay jaws,
    courting her caged canaries;
        Maria admires his timbre.

Her shade glimpses down and waves me
  up. Seated above palms
    and cypresses, olives and *nerantzia,*

we chat all day over spoonfuls of rose-
  petal jam and cool water.
    I notice a pile of men's

underwear on her bare bedroom floor,
  my glance posing the question.
    She answers,

"They belonged to my lover
  who's not coming back."
    "How can you be sure?"

She responds in bel canto: "The saddest thing—
  understanding my motives does not
    change them, whether I speak or sing."

I see myself in her tarnished voice,
  then see myself back
    in my New York apartment,

flanked by friends, the balcony
  a wrought-iron fire escape,
    a pigeon clenching its coil.

Notes

PART ONE

7 × 7th Avenue

Sarx: flesh in ancient Greek.

Touch

Translations of the French phrases in the order of their appearance:

"May I help you?"

"Oh no, sir, I'm simply looking."

"But why are you . . ."

"Sir, don't you wish to buy anything?"

The Heart of the Dauphin

Translation of the popular song:

Would you know / A cuckold, a bastard, a whore? / See the King, the Queen. / And Monsieur the Dauphin.

The rondeau, sung by the ghost, was written by François Villon, translated by John Payne.

Tout chacun c'est le visage de Maman: each one is Mother's face.

Lettres de cachet: orders under the King's seal, whereby detainees were imprisoned for life.

Dieu: God.

l'Église: the Church.

PART TWO

Safety

Naples yellow is a painter's term for a deep cream color.

Translations of the Italian phrases in the order of their appearance:

"In the label."

"I'm sorry, little boy, but I didn't mean to be impolite."

Gate of Ivory, Gate of Horn

Clairvoyee: a window-like hole cut into a hedge.

Worth

Puedo: I can in Spanish.

Octavio Paz's poem "Blanco" (meaning *blank* and *white*) was written on a long scroll of paper.

Eating God

Theophagy: literally *eating God* in Greek.

"I plead with you not to be an unseasonable kindness to me. Allow me to be eaten by beasts through whom I can attain to God," Ignatius to the Romans. *The Gnostic Gospels.*

Health

Hosh: an inner court of an Egyptian house.

Bridging: when fibrosis, or scarring, spreads from the surface to the interior of the liver.

Skeleton light: a lighthouse with an open framework tower.

Writ in Water

Brede: interwoven design on the urn.

Hiding in Intervals
For my father Theodore (1926-1995).
Corot's Red Fleck
Traction fissure: in an old painting, a wide crack that reveals the ground layer beneath.
Spoken Under Hypnosis: An Earlier Life in Burma as a Woman Named Mi Aye
Oliphant: a horn made from an elephant tusk.
Love
Ελλαδα: Greece.
Nerantzia: small, sweet oranges found in mountainous regions of Greece.

Becket Logan

DEAN KOSTOS is a graduate of Antioch University's writing program. He is the author of the collection *The Sentence That Ends with a Comma* (which was taught at Duke University) and the chapbook *Celestial Rust*. He co-edited the anthology *Mama's Boy*, a Lambda Book Award finalist. His poetry has appeared in leading literary magazines, among them *Barrow Street*, *Bloom*, *Boulevard*, *Chelsea*, the *Cimarron Review*, *The James White Review*, the *Paris Review (forthcoming)*, *Poetry New York*, *Rattapallax*, the *Southwest Review*, the *Western Humanities Review*, and elsewhere. His translations from the Modern Greek and co-translations from the Spanish have appeared in *Talisman*, *Bomb*, and *Barrow Street*; his reviews in *American Book Review*, Harvard University Press's Web site, and elsewhere. *Box-Triptych*, his choreopoem, was staged at La Mama. He has taught poetry writing at Pratt University, Gotham Writers' Workshop, Teachers & Writers Collaborative, The Great Lakes Colleges Association, and The Columbia Scholastic Press Association. He is a member of PEN American Center and was also the recipient of a Yaddo fellowship. Trained initially as a visual artist, his works have been exhibited in galleries and at the Brooklyn Museum.

Made in the USA
Monee, IL
07 July 2026